SENT!

to your neighbors

Principles & practices of relational evangelism

James H. Hall

E-mail: JHHalls@aol.com
Web site: www.newchristian.com

ISBN: 061573698X
ISBN-13: 978-0615736983

CONTENTS

*Local leaders and all readers are invited to add local or personal examples of practices presented - in addition to the interactive learning exercises.

INTRODUCTION

Get personal with the Good News

God sent Jesus to the world to be the Good Shepherd (John 10) to *whoever* would choose to follow Him. The common modern idea of a shepherd is one who simply guides and cares for a flock of sheep. Jesus' narrative, however, compares Himself to an ancient Middle Eastern shepherd who cherishes and names every sheep in his flock - and has a unique personal relationship with each one. Each sheep in turn recognizes its name only when spoken by its shepherd and then follows. With His human followers, Jesus relates to each one in a uniquely personal manner that is not exactly the same with any other. It is certainly "amazing grace" that eternal God would continuously give every earthly follower His undistracted personal attention and care.

What also stretches our thinking is to recognize that every individual who is *not* in relationship with Jesus is nonetheless valued by Him as a sheep, who - though separated from Him - still belongs to Him and belongs in the flock (Luke 15:32)! He feels compassion for each lost person because they are "confused and helpless, like sheep (who don't do well) without a shepherd" (Matthew 9:36 NLT). He misses being in relationship with them as the prodigal's Father who feels as if His runaway son is lost and dead (Luke 15:32).

Observe Jesus' urgent pursuit of specific lost sheep in the ways He interacts with Nicodemus (John 3), the Samaritan woman at the well (John 4), the poolside lame man (John 5), the adulterous woman (John 8), the man born blind (John 9), and the rich young ruler (Matthew 19) – to name a few. He did not have a canned "one-size-fits-all" speech for the persons with whom He spoke. Each one recognized that He was relating to them as an individual, as He factored into His conversation His awareness of their life situation and the impact it had left on them. The ways He then lovingly extends Himself to them clearly verifies His reputation of being a "friend of sinners"!

Jesus' example of connecting with individuals was later continued by His disciples-turned-apostles (lit. "sent ones"). We see Peter with Cornelius, Philip with the Ethiopian, scattered saints in Acts 8:1, and Paul describing his varied approach in relating to individuals in I Corinthians 9:19-22, Ephesians 4:29, and Colossians 4:4-6. These reports reflect the value early Christians placed on **conversational interactive witness** with individuals. Their compassionate connecting (without the ease of electronic social networking) resulted in "turning their world upside down". In modern times, believers in Latin America and China have followed suit. The western church is beginning to catch on that we are most fruitful when we **connect with lost people personally and lovingly.**

This booklet is to help you team up with Jesus to change lives forever by delivering His love for and invitation to individual lost sheep in your world – to whom He has sent you (John 17:18; 20:21). All true witnesses to Jesus (Acts 1:8) are sent by Him. By whom and to whom we are sent, and the example and instructions we received from our Sender, should inform and shape our "going into all of (our) world". Let us explore what this means in defining the principles and practices of our mission to the lost sheep already in our personal worlds. The Father, Son, and the Holy Spirit desire them to be found. Do you?

Personal harvest fields

The most accessible and obvious mission field is your neighborhood, your workplace, and the places where you buy and recreate regularly. The word *neighbor* - applied by Jesus to a Samaritan who helped a Jewish stranger – signifies *proximity*, someone within reach. Those who are within reach daily for five days a week – or on a weekly or frequent basis, meet the proximity principle in a greater way than a surprise encounter between strangers on a highway. Jesus says simply, "Show mercy!" to those within our reach (Luke 10:37). He has sent you to deliver to others mercy you have received.

"Neighbors" include persons within reach in the spaces where you already habitually go for your own personal benefit. For example, you have a job location, a house or apartment, maybe a fitness center membership, various stores where you shop – and places for recreation and eating. These are your personal harvest fields.

NOTES: List the places where you regularly spend time.

"Lift up your eyes and look" beyond yourself and notice (John 4:35) – there are *people* in those places who will live forever somewhere! As the Father sent Jesus into your world, in the same manner Jesus has sent you to your "neighbors" in your world (Stop and read John 17:18; 21:22). He doesn't want you to just tolerate them with appropriate courtesies because you are a decent God fearing person. He wants you to love them as Jesus loved you when you weren't giving Him the time of day. The One Who was sent to you is **sending you** to them.

Are you AWOL or on duty? Are you a conduit intentionally sharing your blessings, or a bucket conserving your benefits for yourself? "Lift up your eyes" and see the potential harvest in your world! Don't just "go to work". Go on a "missions trip" every day at your jobsite. Don't just go shopping or go work out with those maintaining their short term health. Go share God's long term goodness with those around you. How does that work? Keep reading!

PHASE ONE:
SENT BY THE GOOD SHEPHERD

Sent by compassion

Compassion for me

How does *my* Shepherd see and feel for *me*? King David of old discovered while he was a shepherd boy that "The Lord is my Shepherd". Underline the words in the following New Testament story excerpts that symbolically refer to you at a stage in your life when *you* were a lost sheep not yet found by the Good Shepherd. Also, [circle] the words that describe how your Shepherd *saw* you and *felt* about you before you were found.

"Jesus went through all the towns and villages...When he saw the crowds, he had compassion on them, because they were harassed and helpless, like sheep without a shepherd" (Matthew 9:35-36 NIV).

"So (the runaway son) got up (from his pigpen) and went to his father. But while he was still a long way off, his father saw him and was filled with compassion for him; he ran to his son...(rejoicing because he) who was dead is now alive, and was lost (but) now is found." (Luke 15:20, 24 NIV)

5

NOTES: Write how you discovered that the Good
Shepherd loved you before you were a "found sheep"?

Compassion for others

How does my Shepherd see and feel for *His* lost sheep in *my* world? Find in the above passages words that refer to persons in your weekly world who are lost sheep. Underline the words that refer to them, and [circle] the words that describe how Jesus *sees* them and *feels* about them. (Are those words already underlined and circled?)

Now underline words or phrases used by Jesus that say how *we* should see, feel, and act toward His lost sheep – looking at the Good Samaritan in the following quote as our example.

"A Samaritan...saw (the beaten man beside the road and) and felt compassion for him. Going over to him (he) soothed his wounds with olive oil and wine and bandaged them. Then he put the man on his own donkey and took him to an inn and took care of him. The next day he handed the innkeeper two silver coins, telling him, 'Take care of this man. If his bill runs higher than this, I'll pay you the next time I am here." (Luke 10:33-35 NLT)

"Love your enemies. Pray for those who persecute you. In that way you will be acting as true children of your Father in heaven. For He gives His sunlight to both the evil and the good, and He sends rain on the just and the unjust alike." (Matt. 5:44-45 NLT)

NOTES on how the Samaritan was like Jesus to the beaten man:

NOTES on how you see and feel for people in your personal harvest fields.

Pray until you begin to see your "neighbors" (ones nearby, wherever they are) through God's eyes, and feel for them with His heart. When this happens, you will

a) *see* their needs more than their faults, and

b) *feel* compassion for their life condition now and what it would be forever without Jesus.

NOTES: What impact do their unmet needs seem to be having on *them*?

Is God helping you see below the surface to know how they are really doing?

Sent with God's gifts

Freely receive, freely give

What God gives you always includes surplus for others. God's will for us on the horizontal plane ("Love your neighbor as yourself" Luke 10:27) flows from His provision to us in our vertical relationship with Him – i.e. I have "freely... received, (so I can) freely give." (Matthew10:8, e.g. Luke 10:27, 33; 11:4)

A) Grace/forgiveness received from God is our resource for forgiving/giving grace to others – i.e. we can love them without requiring them to deserve our love, and in spite of their offenses against us.

B) Friendship with God provides resource for being a friend to others.

C) Leadership from God empowers us to lead others - by example and influence – i.e. others can follow us to Jesus.

In PHASE 2, we will look at how to deliver these resources to others through the natural ways that people interact with each other – with *listening, words, actions* and *emotions* (Luke 10:34-37; Galatians 5:22-23).

But first - to help us supernaturally deliver to others what is provided to us - Jesus gives us ability to be witnesses through being filled with the Holy Spirit. Let us examine this gift from Jesus (Luke 24:49) for the sake of receiving this power and to also be able to help others receive.

Ability from above

Jesus said the Spirit empowered Him to give blessings to others (Luke 4:18). Jesus also said: "You shall receive power (ability), after the Spirit is come upon you, and you will be my witnesses." (Acts 1:8) His plan is for us to *team up* with the Spirit to represent Jesus. (Matthew 10:19-20; Acts 4:29-31; 8:4) Read carefully these passages and see if you have any doubt remaining that God wants to empower you to live a life that is an effective witness to Jesus.

How to receive

Acts 2:4 tells how the disciples experienced this filling when they surrendered to the Spirit so deeply that they praised God in words that the Spirit gave them. When you surrender to the Spirit and are filled in the same way, you will also pray with words the Spirit gives you – in a manner beyond your natural ability. This will give you faith to team up with the Spirit to be a witness in deeds and words beyond your own ability.

To be filled with the Spirit, you need to surrender to the Spirit. Ask Jesus to show you if you are holding back from the Spirit's control in daily life in any way that will hinder your being filled with the Holy Spirit – and what you should do about it. Promise God you will do what He says, and tell someone who will hold you accountable to follow through on what you promised God.

Now ask Jesus to fill you with His Holy Spirit. Your part is to surrender completely so the Spirit can take control. Begin to surrender your voice – with that unruly tongue! (James 3:2-12) – in praising Jesus out loud with joy (Luke

24:52-53) because He has saved you and is going to fill you (being "filled" the first time is the same as being "baptized") with His Holy Spirit. He promised (Luke 11:9-13; Acts 2:38-39) – so thank Him, because you trust Him to do what He says - knowing He will fill you!

As you praise Him, concentrate completely on Jesus the Baptizer (John 1:33). He will make you know in your heart (give you FAITH) that if you will begin to speak, the Spirit will give you the words to say. (Acts 2:4: "They began to speak...as the Spirit was giving them (words).") When the faith comes, you begin to speak – but don't use your own words. Just relax and say whatever the Spirit gives you to say. Your praying language will include sentences you will not understand, but words from the Spirit will flow easily – as you provide your voice to be used by the Spirit to speak His words. Remember that Acts 2:4 says "*They spoke*, as the Spirit gave the words." It was a team effort between the Spirit and each individual.

Teamwork

As you frequently pray this supernatural way, it will soon feel very natural - so continue to pray this way daily! The more you and the Holy Spirit team up to pray beyond your natural ability, the more you will receive ability to witness with His help beyond your natural ability. In your witness conversations there will be times when you will be amazed at the words that flow out of your mouth that you know are beyond your natural ability or knowledge – obviously by the help of the Spirit. And the impact of your words will be evidence of the Spirit's power as well. I am sure Peter was amazed to hear himself preach on the Day of Pentecost (Acts 2:14) and see the results, after several verbal low points he had experienced in preceding weeks!

Sent already

As was already said, Jesus has already sent you into your harvest fields – to the persons with whom you are in regular contact who are not following Him. Jesus is saying: "I tell you, open your eyes and look at the fields. They are ripe for harvest" (John 4:35). Write names of people in your world who don't seem to follow Jesus.

FAMILY

NEIGHBORHOOD

1. _____   1._____

2. _____   2. _____

3. _____   3. _____

4. _____   4. _____

EMPLOYMENT/ SCHOOL   RECREATION

1. _____   1._____

2. _____   2. _____

3. _____   3. _____

4. _____   4. _____

Ask God to show you from the above four fields, up to

4 FRIENDS 4 PRAYER & 4 FRIENDSHIP

to whom He is specifically sending you. Write their names below. Pray that God will fill your heart with love for them. Also pray for them! (Note: Your "four friends" could include new believers who need discipling.)

4 Friends List

1. _____   Notes re hindrances to faith

2. _____   for which to intercede:

3. _____

4. _____

Keep in focus the goal of being a witness. Your mission is to help lost sheep stand at the end of time in the crowd-of-the-found. There will also be a bigger crowd-of-the-lost. Every human ever born in the history of mankind will one day stand in one of these two crowds described in Revelation 7:9-12; 20:11f.

NOTES: Summarize in your own words these two scenes:

Every person you see repeatedly in the course of your everyday life – from the nicest to the most obnoxious, will stand in one of these crowds.

God wants to use you to make a difference in where they will stand and live forever. He has sent you into their world to help influence them to make a choice for which they will eternally give thanks. Are you "about your Father's business" – or ready to get started, or restart? **A passion to reach the lost – compassion - should be central to the heart of all who call themselves genuine followers of Christ.** (Mark 1:17) If you are low on compassion, pray until…

James H Hall

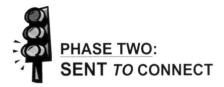

PHASE TWO:
SENT *TO* CONNECT

So for the sake of loving, look for ways to bridge the natural relational gap with your neighbors (those nearby) in your life. Also look for ways that Jesus *already* has been working in them. (John 4:38; 5:19) He will send you where He is already at work, to join Him in harvest labor. See the amazingly simple game plan that Jesus followed, as He explained in John 5:19:

"The Son can do nothing by himself. He does only what he sees the Father doing. Whatever the Father does, the Son also does."

Be sensitive to what the Holy Spirit is already doing in persons you know, and stay tuned to what and when the Spirit will prompt you to do or say something they need to receive at just the right time for them to receive it. God's timing is perfect, so "pay attention" to His leading!

NOTES: Have there been any recent promptings or stirrings by the Holy Spirit in you to do or say something specific to someone in your world?

Actions speak before words

Indirect statements

Being a witness begins in our hearts with Jesus' compassion for specific lost persons, and then translates outwardly into compassionate behavior. Prior to compassion in action, however, is the message our general actions send when not directed specifically at the persons we want to win over to Christ. Turning on the charm when targeting a potential new disciple smacks of natural salesmanship. Especially in your workplace, your coworkers should gather from your attitudes, actions, and everyday speech the impression that you are a bit - or a lot - unusual. Would it not be reasonable that the God of the universe personally present in you and helping you with your attitudes and actions would create some kind of impression on those around you?

Think how much a person's behavior, body language and "vibes" play a part in others' impressions of them! You may not think of yourself as a high impact person, but the One living in you certainly is! And He has ways of making His presence felt through you! Think about it! **You bring Almighty God's presence into your work space!** It is the continuation of the Incarnation described in John 1: "The Word became human and lived among us." We are Christ's body, His physical being going to work at your jobsite! What a privilege, to "introduce" the King of the Universe to your co-workers – who loves them and who they desperately need, whether they know it or not! Some do know.

The first major factor in the impression you make at work, is *how* you work. Christ followers should be known for the principle: "If a job is worth doing, it is worth doing well!" Paul urges us in Colossians 3:23: "Whatever you do, work at it with all your heart, as working for the Lord, not for human masters." Notice this does not mean you have to have superior skill when you do a task, but that you put your heart into your work and do your personal best – even when no other humans are watching. Jesus is watching – especially since you should be relying on His "ever present help" in doing the task!

How you relate to authority over you in the workplace also sends a loud message to those in authority and to coworkers. And if you are in a management or any kind of decision making position, make it clear Who you primarily answer to for your decisions. My good friend David Robinson refers to making "everyday decisions that reveal who we really are when the pressure is on and our decisions have significant consequences?" (*Idle in the Marketplace*, City Limits International Publishing, 2012; p.35)

How you treat those "under" you is also important. Paul writes in Ephesians 6:8-10: "You know that the Lord will reward each one for whatever good they do, whether they are slave or free. And masters, treat your slaves in the same way. Do not threaten them, since you know that he who is both their Master and yours is in heaven, and there is no favoritism with him."

Direct statements

And finally, there is the issue of how you relate directly to fellow workers. They are your immediate neighbors in your workplace and our mandate and mission is to "Love (our) neighbor as (ourselves)." Neighborly love is generally delivered best to coworkers according to friendship principles (cf. Jesus the "friend of sinners".) Begin with questions about the other person's interests, well-being and family – and some humor. Listen to their answers with genuine interest – and ask follow up questions for clarification.

If you are a patient listener and try to understand the other person, it builds a caring bridge with them. Look for needs and unanswered questions for which Jesus can provide. I like the saying: "Jesus is the answer, so what is your question?" Jesus is most obviously relevant to unbelievers when His presence is applied to meeting their daily needs. Very often, the Spirit arranges things so that their struggles and questions are similar to needs Jesus has met for you. His answers for you can be shared with them when the Spirit prompts you to do so. Hearing your reports of everyday experiences with Jesus begins to show them **how a daily relationship with Jesus works.** Most unbelievers are now-focused more than long range planners and so are more interested in current benefit from Jesus over settling the future issue of life after death.

As they observe and interact with you, they can begin to pick up on the attitude of hope you have – immediate *and* long term. Many unbelievers have a bleak long term outlook and a present deep hollow feeling, but they avoid thinking about those issues by staying focused on current amusements and concerns. The sense of peace they pick up in Christians, especially during believers' times of crisis and loss, is often a powerful witness. Our adult son's journey with congenital heart issues has opened countless doors for sharing the faith that was sustaining us. Historical times of hardship were the context of Peter's words: "Always be prepared to give an answer to everyone who asks you to give the reason for the hope that you have. But do this with gentleness and respect." (I Peter 3:15 NIV)

Notice that Peter says our manner in sharing the Good News is also important. Paul says that gracious and seasoned speech will enable us to "know how to *respond* (my emphasis) to each person" – implying that they have initiated the exchange. Our answers should not be "canned" responses but rather designed to fit "each person" to whom we are speaking (Colossians 4:5-6). Let us now look more closely at how to communicate the essential Good News of Jesus to your lost friends.

A kindly manner opens doors

You are the host

Insecurity and resulting nervousness are frequent for the beginner in trying to verbally share the Good News. It may be helpful to see yourself as a host who is offering hospitality – acceptance, engaging conversation, and a kindly manner to set the other person at ease. Even though we as believers are aliens in this world, we can still feel very much at home in our own skin. Remind yourself – you are a servant doing the will of the King of the Universe, a sheep following the Great Shepherd, a child secure in God's forever family who is obeying his or her Father. How much more God-confidence can we ask for? We are the prodigals who have "come home" – stray sheep who have been found – and we are inviting wandering prodigals to come in out of the cold! Remember, for many of them it is still "a jungle out there." So be comfortable in reaching out to those who need Jesus!

Notice how Jesus – from out of town - was the host in the conversation with the Samaritan woman at her hometown well. He surprised her by requesting a drink, risking rejection as He was in a hostile neighborhood. His initiative resulted in saving faith for the nearby village. Philip - a lone traveler - was the host to the Ethiopian official in his limo and entourage returning from Jerusalem. After eaves dropping on the official's Scripture reading, he took the risky initiative to offer him explanation, an offer that resulted in the official's salvation and many others in his homeland. Then there is the famous connection between the Samaritan on his way to Jericho for business who became the host to offer help to the beaten Jewish man by the road. The Jew readily accepted the offer from one whom Jewish culture viewed as an alien low life – who definitely would not be typically viewed as a welcoming host!

Walk your dog

You can discover door openers with neighbors on your street (e.g. shared interests like pets, sports, hobbies or clean jokes) by looking for opportunities for casual contact. Be warm and open and ready to listen. Show interest in getting acquainted by asking questions – then listen and respond to what you hear. Don't be in a hurry to proclaim the Gospel message. Look for opportunities to respond to an obvious need, a reported need, or a Spirit-revealed need. A very simple and often appreciated response is to promise to pray for the need expressed. Be sensitive to the Spirit prompting you to offer to pray with them for the need at that moment. And it is okay to calmly pray with eyes open, if the unbeliever seems more comfortable with that.

Be on the lookout for evidence of spiritual thirst - a desire in the person without Christ for more in life than what they are currently experiencing. (Remember, **no one is truly satisfied without Christ**, no matter how good a front they put on!) When their significant questions are expressed, calmly explain how Jesus is the Answer to their question or need - or you can tell how Jesus has been your answer to a similar need in your own life. Be patient and wait for opportunities to open up naturally or be created by the Spirit. Sometimes the Spirit will nudge you to say something specific even when there does not seem to be an opportunity.

If you are presented with a tough philosophical question for which you don't have an answer, don't hesitate to say "I don't have an answer to that one." But keep in mind that a person with an experience is never at the mercy of a person with an argument. At the same time, don't hesitate to get involved in philosophical discussions. Scripture holds up very well under honest academic and philosophical scrutiny.

Walk your talk

As mentioned above, the Holy Spirit will open doors with neighbors in whom He has already been working, and to whom He has previously sent a witness or witnesses to deliver to them some benefits from or influence toward God. This is the plowing of the ground of the heart that helps turn it into "good soil" that is receptive to the seed of the Gospel. Notice the labor that the Spirit had done previously through someone in the Samaritan village of Sychar (see John 4:37-38), through the angel with

Cornelius, through the Scripture with the Ethiopian, and through Jesus Himself appearing to Paul – before the sent human witnesses entered their world.

With previous influence that God has sent, and with the present action of the Spirit, unbelieving neighbors' hearts are inspired to trust you enough to crack the door for sincere communication. As they interact with you and sense the warmth and welcome of God's love radiating from you, they will often become receptive to you – to the message of your actions and attitudes, and eventually to the Gospel as well.

There often is a spiritual awareness they don't understand that is God tugging at their heart, and giving them a spiritual hunger similar to a starving person smelling fresh baked bread. The Father is "drawing them" – without which no one can come to Christ. (John 4:7; Acts 8:26-31; 10:19-20) This working of the soil creates hunger and receptivity in the lost person - in contrast to the reaction to the combative spirit that often emanates from "bold" witnesses who win arguments and lose friends. Occasionally there is a place for confrontational witness – but not usually, especially with "neighbors" you see regularly.

"Jesus in me loves you"

Where there is opportunity for ongoing relationship, pursue a trusting friendship bond with unbelievers in your regular world that may take time to develop. Jesus certainly modeled this as reported in Luke 15:1-2 and other Gospel passages. Ask the Spirit to guide you in seeking repeated friendly contacts over a period of time and showing practical love as the Spirit leads you and provides genuine compassion through you to respond to specific needs. Non-Christians may be surprised at or suspicious of your motivation in extending yourself, because of the self-centeredness of most people and themselves. So be patient.

Persist peacefully in reaching out, and allow the Spirit to convince them that His caring through you is genuine. Also look for "common ground" – i.e. conversational topics of shared interest and shared activities (a ballgame, fishing, lunch or coffee or a backyard BBQ, workout, run/walk for exercise, etc.) through which you can cultivate friendship and allow for unhurried conversations.

Conversations: road to conversion

Having gained entrance to their world through some degree of trusted friendship, you can begin the process of *interactive* communication of Good News. There are *facts that lost people must have* to enable them to entrust their lives to Jesus Christ. The most effective means of breaking up the "hard ground" of those who "hear the word but do not understand" (Matthew 13:19) is through friendly conversation – usually conversation*s* (plural) – so persist patiently.

Conversation is by definition two-way communication – which allows you to assess whether a person is in fact understanding the Good News as you share it, or is just acting polite while you talk. The *only* **way to confirm comprehension** is when the person with whom you are speaking **says back to you what they think you mean.** When the witness does most or all of the talking, the recipient often does not understand what is said. An effective witness must take time to listen to informal feedback to know if the Good News is being understood. The primary characteristic of "good soil" in Matthew 13:23 is represented by those who "truly hear and understand" – which enables them to eventually bear much fruit.

Conversation is also helpful to determine whether the response to the message is the "immediate" and "with joy" acceptance associated by Jesus with rocky soil where there is shallow dirt and little root – followed by "immediate" falling away when problems and persecution comes. The Good News was misinterpreted as a quick fix for life's problems and is discarded when it doesn't make life easy for the new "believer" who is trying out the Gospel.

Conversation can also help clarify that the Gospel is not simply an offer of a helping hand from God that can be accessed when desired. Devotion to Christ must be given priority over competing worries and the pursuit of money. There is a counting of the cost that is called for in a sincere response that causes one to "take up his cross" and follow. Christ must be viewed as "Lord of all" or He is not "lord at all". (e.g. rich young ruler)

Conversations with non-followers don't guarantee a fruitful response, but they go a long way toward preparing a receptive person's mind and heart for a sincere and fruitful response to the Gospel. I believe this is why **person-to-person conversation, the primary means of communicating the Gospel in New Testament times**, is still and always the *best method* of informing lost persons of their one hope and inviting them to enter into a trust relationship with Jesus! And conversation is the only method that *every* believer can employ to make the Good News accessible to those they meet – a behavior that is also *expected of every believer!* (Acts 1:8)

PHASE THREE:
SENT TO INTRODUCE THE SENDER

Know what a lost person needs to know

The first step in effective communication of the Good News is to have a clear grasp of the content of the "news" that every lost person needs to know. This is an issue of eternal life or eternal death – and falls into two categories:

1) **Information** about earthly and eternal life with Jesus and His basic benefits – to awaken *desire* to accept God's offer.

2) **Invitation** to accept God's offer and *start* living the new life in partnership with Jesus – who is the Source of all blessing and Lord (authority) over all of one's personal life.

Invitation should usually not be offered until there is evidence the non-follower is beginning to believe the Gospel information. So let us review first the basic information about new life with Jesus and its benefits and requirements.

Prepare to begin with brief summary statements, and then elaborate if interest is shown. Don't try to force a conversation if resistance or disinterest is evident. If you do, it makes the listener feel like you are forcing your way through the door of their comfort zone. Stick to the amount of space they are giving you, after you "knock" and talk on their "doorstep". Don't make them feel like you are trying to "break and enter"! Go only as far as you are invited – unless prompted by the Spirit to "push" the issue, and then do so kindly and calmly. Sometimes it is conviction (guilt) that is creating their resistance. But be sure it is the Spirit pushing *you*, especially if you naturally enjoy confrontation.

INFORMATION (Good news for everyone, everywhere!)

God's eternal benefits

God's **great gift** to mankind is not primarily a fire escape, as important as that is. Above all it is an **eternal *personal* relationship** with **Himself** that begins on earth and continues forever. It is similar to a perfect earthly parent-child relationship.

The Lord's Prayer begins with "Our Father" (Matthew 6:9). John 1:12 states that we can become "children of God". Romans 8:15-17 shows that God intends that relationship to be warm and loving ("Abba" is similar to a respectful "Daddy"), with two-way communication. Every real relationship has two-way "traffic" – *interaction* of deeds and words and feelings that travel back and forth between the ones in the relationship. God "first loved us", and offers to us relationship, as summarized in John 3:16; 1:12; 15:14.

(Note that care should be given to clarify the kind of Father God is, in light of the negative experiences of many children in our world with their earthly fathers.) This relationship with heavenly Father is through His eternal Son Jesus Christ, whom His Father sent to earth to become human flesh, live on earth, purchase salvation, conquer physical death, and then return to heaven. So the first and ongoing point of reference for **receiving eternal**

life on earth is through this **unique man in history who is also God, Jesus Christ.** Just the mention of His name inspires attraction toward Him or reaction against Him! There is no middle ground of indifference toward the Christ of God. The Good News (Gospel) can be summarized as follows:

A) Jesus **forgives** us for our disobedience and disrespect of Him as holy and ruling God – who created us to live according to His purpose for our lives. God sent His Son Jesus to earth to become a perfect sinless person and suffer the punishment that God's justice demands for our self-will and rebellion against God. This allows God to forgive us, if we ask for forgiveness based on trusting in Jesus' suffering the punishment we deserve (equivalent of eternal hell) for every bad thing we have done and will do. In other words, He paid our fine or served the equivalent of our eternal prison sentence for sin.

Benefit: Through faith in Jesus, we are now free from being punished with eternal death for sin, and free from being controlled by sin in our earthly behavior! So while we are still tempted to sin, but we can resist and not sin with Jesus' help. We can also be forgiven for sins we commit when we ask. (This explains how Jesus is the "Sacrifice" for our sins. See John 3:16.)

B) Jesus becomes our heavenly **Friend,** beginning while we are on earth and lasting forever. For everyone who invites Him, He comes to live *inside of* them, to always be with them. He pays attention to everything about that person – and desires ongoing two-way conversation through the Bible and through prayer. He gives practical help as needed, in response to our requests (prayers) and often just based on the good He wants for us.

Benefit: When we accept His friendship we rely on Him because He is always with us and pays attention to us and to our prayers. We focus on Him and listen to Him. We express our love and requests to Him (prayers) and trust Him to help us to obey Him and to provide what we need. (This is Jesus as "Savior" [One who rescues]. John 1:12; 3:16.)

C) Jesus becomes our Leader and requires our cooperation. He leads us through His written Word, His example while on earth, and His Spirit who lives in us and talks with us. He partners with us to help us **follow** His path and plan for each moment of each day. He has a purpose for our earthly and eternal life.

Benefit: He will personally guide us to fulfill His plan for each day – if we pay attention to Him and obey what we believe He is telling us to do in the Bible and by His Spirit giving us instructions. (This is Jesus as our "Lord" [Authority]. John 15:14.)

So as God's children, we receive the loving benefits from God as He responds to our faith in Him through Jesus Christ. His love extended to us can be summarized with the words *forgive, friend,* and *follow.* We respond to Jesus loving us first when we:

A) Ask Him to forgive us for all our disobedience, with great gratitude for taking on Himself the punishment we deserve.

B) Believe and trust in Him as our eternal friend to provide whatever we need, when we need it.

C) Cooperate with Him and follow Him daily as our lead partner.

All this can happen only as we communicate with and depend on Jesus who is always with us. (John 15:4-5,14)

All the components of the information in the above section should be clear and easily brought up and explained by you - the witness – as opportunities arise in conversations or as prompted by the Spirit. In most conversations early in your relationship, it would be an overload to introduce all at once the whole plan of salvation. After you have shared all the components in multiple conversations, you can then review the whole plan in a single conversation. However, the main thing is to do as the Spirit prompts you to do.

Introduce Jesus in you (this is huge!)

Daily news

When friends talk, they usually include news about recent experiences in their life and other people's experiences they have heard about. For followers of Jesus, there should always be something "happening" in their lives related to Jesus. Look for opportunities to bring casual reports of Jesus' activity in your life and other people's lives into normal conversation. Keep the above ABC categories of benefits in mind and look for opportunities to tell about recent experiences in those categories in **your own life** as follows:

A) Behavior that resulted in you asking Jesus to forgive you. (e.g. an unkind comment to a family member or coworker that required asking forgiveness from Jesus *and* the person you offended.)

B) Ways Jesus has been a friend to you. (e.g. How Jesus provided during unemployment or comforted after losing a loved one. It could also be something like finding a good sale on a needed item when funds were tight, or a kind word from someone when you were down.)

C) Ways that Jesus guided you. (e.g. Jesus showing you a bad attitude through reading Scripture about the fruit of the Spirit, or receiving peace about a choice between two job offers or a decision to do a kind deed.)

NOTES: Write a personal example from each category. The Spirit may open a door soon to repeat one of your recorded experiences as a response to a coworker or neighbor or workout partner saying "How are you doing?"

A)

B)

C)

This will begin to inform your unbelieving friends that having Jesus in your life as a Friend guides and benefits your whole life here on earth in things both big and small. Being a "Christian" is not just about repeating a prayer for eternal life insurance. As an unbelieving friend begins to compare the benefits you are experiencing with the lack of those benefits in their life, the Spirit will begin to draw or tug on their heart to believe and benefit as you do. Your everyday life testimonies also inform them of **how faith works in day to day living** (pre-conversion discipling). This explains the kinds of faith they will need to commit to for them to have their own daily relationship with Jesus.

As unbelievers around you watch your life and interact with you, usually they will begin to have questions about what you have and how and why. Again, remember I Peter 3:15-16 (NLT): "If someone asks about your Christian hope, always be ready to explain it. But do this in a gentle and respectful way. Keep your conscience clear. Then if people speak against you, they will be ashamed when they see what a good life you live because you belong to Christ."

Offer to pray

Let your friendship grow through open and honest communication, without trying to appear different than what you really are. Life's issues will come up naturally – or supernaturally - in conversation. Find out what their questions and needs are, and then present Jesus as their Answer to those specific issues. Let your words be "good for edification according to the need of the moment, that (they) may give grace to those who hear." (Ephesians 4:29 NASB) In Colossians 4:6, Paul tells us that gracious speech helps us "know how to respond to each person." Relate how Jesus has helped in your own life with similar issues. Relax and trust the Spirit to guide you and nudge you regarding when and what to say - "as the Spirit gives you words".

Depend on the Holy Spirit to help you influence your friends in ways that are appropriate to the stage of their journey to Jesus. When your unbelieving friends share problems they are facing, promise to pray for God to help them – even offer to pray right then in their presence. (An "eyes-open" prayer is fine, if you sense it will be more comfortable for an unchurched person.)

When eating out and your server brings your food, ask if you can include a need of theirs in your prayer. If they linger, include them in giving the prayer. (Their response usually includes gratitude!) Leave a generous tip and add a well-written tract! If your funds are tight, drink water to save on your bill and free up funds for the tip – a small sacrifice to plow the soil of your server's heart to be more receptive to the seed of the Gospel from you or others. (Sadly, "Christians" are often wait-help's least favorite kind of people to serve – based on their lack of courtesy and minimal tipping!)

Praying *with* a friend or neighbor about a need they have shared is often welcomed by hurting people and often brings a surprising – to the unbeliever - powerful sense of God's presence in the moment. (I prayed with a neighbor at 10 PM in his driveway for his wife in the hospital just after he arrived home from work. I just "happened" to be putting out my trash containers for pick up the next morning when he pulled in across the street.) Later inquire about the need, assuring them that you are still praying. Encourage them to also pray about it. Pray also for their decisions, their families, their successes, their earthly relationships, in addition to their relationship with God. (I Timothy 2:1)

This kind of interaction sends a repeated message that **God wants to be involved in the details of their everyday lives in a very personal way** – and how that works. It is also an act of caring on your part, and usually appreciated by non-Christians. Everyone knows in their hearts that they need "outside help". Through friendship, you will allow unbelievers to **experience Jesus in you and with you** (the fruit of the Spirit) that will help them to desire to have their own relationship with Jesus. You have been introducing Jesus in your life, before asking them to invite Him into theirs.

Helpful tips

Use easy language ("Make it *clear...*" Colossians 4:3-4)

When the time comes to explain the Gospel "contract", be sure to use language that is guaranteed to be clear and honest to a non-churched person.

NOTES: Practice clear speech ahead of time by writing out an explanation of the Gospel without using any "Christianese". Think of an unchurched person you know, and consider his or her age, education, culture, etc. Consciously write to that person, using simple terms that they will easily and clearly understand (e.g. housewife, businessman, young person, child, elderly person, etc. You might even ask that person to evaluate your attempt and advise you for clarity.). This will be more difficult to do than you expect. Remember, natural eloquence doesn't convict – only the Spirit – so just concentrate on being clear!

Avoid argument. Be comfortable with the unbeliever expressing disagreement with the Bible. Just aim at making clear what the Bible says, and allow the Holy Spirit to do His part of persuading that the Gospel is true. (See Colossians 4:3-4.) If you run out of time in the situation (e.g. "break time" at work is over), just pick up later where you left off.

Be aware that often serious inquirers will welcome meeting to **study the Bible to see what it says about Jesus and faith in Him.** Discipling lessons created for new believers (e.g. *StartUp Studies*) can also be used to inform them of the Bible's definition of a follower of Jesus and clarify the kind of commitments that Jesus asks of them. Serious thinkers often prefer to "look before they leap" and welcome a degree of pre-conversion discipling. Jesus warned about the "shallow dirt and little root" pitfall (Matthew 13:20-21) experienced by those who make an overly impulsive decision - sometimes encouraged by Gospel salespersons. Jesus urges us to "count the cost" before deciding to follow (Luke 14:28f).

Convincing is not your job

Discuss Gospel truths in a peaceful and cheerful manner, using simple and clear words. Again, avoid technical Bible terms like "salvation, repentance, righteousness, have eternal life". Don't try to persuade – that is not your job. (A big relief!) Trust the Holy Spirit to do the persuading. In a kindly way, you can help unbelievers recognize and admit their need, depending on the Spirit to convince them that they have indeed offended Almighty God, and that they are separated from Him and need Jesus payment and forgiveness for their sin. (John 16:8)

An important step: Ask the non-follower to repeat back to you their understanding of each kind of faith needed in a relationship with Jesus, as you review each one. Have them describe their understanding of any particular point or issue you aren't sure they have grasped clearly. This will inform you of the accuracy of their understanding and will often reveal points of confusion or omission that you can clarify. Remember - it is always important to read and understand a contract *before* you sign it!

Don't "soft pedal" parts of Gospel truth that you think might not be acceptable to an unbeliever. Remember, it is your job to communicate clearly and confirm with feedback, and it is the Holy Spirit's role to persuade unbelievers to begin to believe in their spirit that the Gospel is true. It is also His responsibility to draw them to accept God's loving offer of an eternal relationship. (Matthew 16:17) Attraction to Jesus will begin to happen in your friend's heart, as she **sees and feels Jesus in you**, and **hears about Jesus from you and from the Bible**, and begins to feel the **internal tug of the Holy Spirit.**

James H Hall

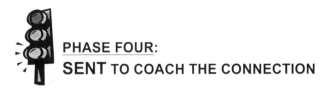

PHASE FOUR:
SENT TO COACH THE CONNECTION

INVITATION

When you see unbelievers leaning toward belief in the truth of the Gospel, invite them to put their trust in Jesus for their whole life now and for their forever future. Encourage but don't pressure. If their response is positive, review the terms of a salvation contract with Lord Jesus Christ.

Facilitate the contract signing

Understand the Contract

Use the following version of the previous ABC outlines for "talking points" to guide your explanation and *invitation to accept Jesus* into an eternal trust relationship, as guided by **John 3:16; 1:12; 15:14.**

Ask Jesus to **forgive** you, trusting Him as your sin-payment. (John 3:16)

Jesus was God's Son Who came to earth and lived a perfect life as a human. He was then punished with physical death and suffering by God the Father as if He (Jesus) had committed every person's wrong doing in violation of God's will. Then Jesus was raised to life and overcame death for mankind and offers eternal life to every person who will receive Him.

If a person will ask Jesus to forgive all of their disrespect and disobedience, God will accept Jesus' personal suffering as payment for what they owe for their sin. The sentence of eternal separation and punishment for their sin has been removed. Also, the power of sin over that person is broken. He or she is no longer compelled by their natural self to disobey God. Temptations will come, but they are no longer a slave to sin. God will help them change.

Believe in (receive) Jesus as your eternal **Friend.** (John 3:16; 1:12)

Eternal relationship is launched when a person invites Jesus to come live inside as eternal Friend, beginning now. Jesus will pay attention every moment to everything about that person. He listens every moment for them to talk to Him, and they can depend on Him for every kind of help.

Contract to cooperate with (**follow**) Jesus as your Leader. (John 15:14)

A prayer promising to follow Jesus is like signing a contract to follow a new Leader. It is putting one's life "under new management", with intent to obey the new Manager. That person can depend on Jesus as Friend to provide the help they need to obey Jesus as Leader ("Lord").

An *eternal* relationship actually begins when the unbeliever's heart **bows to the authority of Jesus**. Faith in a leader is demonstrated by willingness to follow, so unbelief changes to faith in Jesus as "Lord" when the decision is made to give up authority over one's personal life and yield to Jesus' authority.

Depend on the Spirit to guide you in explaining, usually a little at a time, the basic content of the Gospel and how to begin to experience the life it promises and Jesus provides. Encourage the non-believer to begin to ask God for help with everyday issues of life – and see what answers come. Jesus is still a "friend of sinners" and often will answer prayers prior to a conversion commitment to show His love to them.

Remove false barriers

Each of the principles in the ABC outline explained above address common barriers presented by Satan to block faith in Christ. These are:

1. "I've sinned too much for too long. God wouldn't forgive me now." Assure them that Jesus' sin-payment does indeed cover *all* their sins, so they *can* ask Him to forgive. (I John 1:9)

2. "I'd like to change, but I can't. I'm in too deep." Assure them that Jesus their Friend will help them as they put forth effort to make whatever changes He wants them to make. They can come to Him as they are, and He will set them free from the control of their sinful actions, habits, and impulses. He will also continue to forgive their sins as needed. (Romans 6:5-13; Ephesians 2:10)

3. "God has forgiven me and loves me like I am, so I don't need to change. Since I am forgiven, I can go to heaven like I am." Be clear that being a follower of Jesus means putting one's life "under new management", intending to live His way instead of having "my way". No one reaches perfection, but one must intentionally cooperate with Jesus' leadership in everyday living and continue to change for the better. (Romans 6:1-23) To reject this

process is to insult God Almighty and presume to receive His benefits while refusing His requirements.

Help them sign the contract

Remember that salvation must be freely chosen by the recipient, so don't be overly persuasive or pressuring regarding receiving Christ. It is *their* decision! However, when a person is ready to step over the line of faith to follow Jesus, they often need assistance with this death-to-life step. Recommended assistance is as follows:

1. Review the ABC truths that you have discussed and clarified. These truths explain how to begin and continue in an eternal relationship with God through Jesus Christ. That relationship must start here on earth.

2. Ask if they understand/believe/agree with each segment of truth presented. Discuss any questions or reservations they may have. In many parts of the world, a faith commitment to Jesus brings physical danger and social rejection, so a faith commitment to Christ should be taken very seriously.

3. Explain that they need to tell God they have decided to trust Him with their life from now on – based on their faith in Him as stated by these truths. If they mean in their heart what they say to God, He will know it and accept their prayer as honest and sincere. He sees it as them "opening the door" after hearing His voice and His knock, and He will come into their life as He promised He would. (Revelation 3:20)

4. Review the ABC truths as the guide to their prayer, and then encourage the convinced seeker to go ahead and talk to Jesus in their own words. Explain that they need to **tell**

Jesus they have decided to trust Him for His forgiveness, for His friendship, and for following Him daily. Jesus' response will be to accept him or her as a child of the one true God and come to live forever inside of them.

After they have prayed, welcome the new follower to God's eternal family as a new brother or sister! A "Happy Birthday!" is in order.

Conduct under contract (follow-up)

Offer to begin to **meet with them weekly** to give them personal help (discipling) in learning to live each day in conversation and cooperation with Jesus. Encourage them that they "have a great life ahead – not always easy, but always worth the effort"! Remind them that heaven is certain as their final destination – as long as they continue to trust and follow Jesus Christ.

Use the *StartUp Studies - Discipleship for the New Believer* lessons for at least the first month of mentoring the new believer. Your copy is included as the second half of this book. You will need to obtain a separate copy of *StartUp Studies* for the new believer. This can be obtained from www.newchristian.com.

The SUS lessons have the same content as Sessions 1-2 in *THRIVE – A Handbook for New Christians**. So after you mentor the new believer through SUS, begin with Session 3 in the THRIVE manual and continue mentoring for at least six months. Then coach the discipled new believer in winning and discipling others.

*THRIVE – also by James H. Hall - can be ordered at www.newchristian.com

STARTUP
STUDIES

TurnAround Lesson
Friendship Discipling

The New Testament teaches that the Holy Spirit will give internal promptings and external opportunities to be friends with lost persons, and also to be *discipling friends* with those who receive Him! The instructions are, "Disciple all the nations...teaching them to obey all that I have commanded you!" (Matthew 28:18-20)

God intends His family to feel the way He does about new family members (Luke 15:32) and work with Him to disciple them until they are able to:

- walk and talk personally with God,

- hear God speak through the Bible, and

- be witnesses, lead others to Christ, and disciple new believers. (Matthew 28:18-20).

INTRODUCTION

God intends for us to show that we value our new brothers and sisters (Luke 15:32; Acts 11:23). As discipling friends, we should:

1. Celebrate their birth along with God. (Acts 11:23)

2. Accept them as family. (Luke 15:32)

3. Be a friend to them, affirming them and encouraging them to stay faithful to God. (Acts 11:23)

4. Work with them to learn to communicate and cooperate with Jesus. (Matthew 28:19-20)

DISCIPLING

1. **Preparation:** If you haven't done these lessons, study them and write in answers. Discuss each lesson with a friend, to practice verbalizing in everyday vocabulary what you discover in Scripture.. Bring filled-in lessons to discipling meetings for reference during discussion.

2. **Process:** One Discipler with one new believer is recommended. If there are many new believers, groups of two to six can meet with one Discipler. However, individual contacts should be made in person or by phone between meetings, to check on new believers and to encourage the growth of friendship.

   Meet regularly at a place and time convenient to the new believer. Disciplers should be faithful and persistent. New believers' lives depend on these meetings! You do not need to complete a lesson each time. At times you may need to depart from the lesson to deal with pressing needs in new believers' lives. Give them time to understand and apply truth to their lives, but hold them accountable for making sincere effort to obey what they are learning from Scripture. Biblical discipleship means training (discipling) new believers to walk with God in *DAILY FELLOWSHIP* and *OBEDIENCE*, which includes them being Discipling Friends to others. Jesus said, "Teach **THEM** to do all that I have commanded **YOU**." (Matt. 28:20)

3. **First Meeting:** Go through Lesson 1 with the new believer, helping them understand what the lesson means and how it applies to daily living. Pray together without hurry, encouraging the new believer to talk to God out loud as naturally as talking to a person. When

you pray, use simple words so the new believer can learn to pray by listening to you. Make assignments and plans called for, and plan to meet once or twice each week. Try to complete one *StartUP Study* each week, but go at a slower pace if needed by the new believer.

4. **Second Meeting:** Ask about things learned in Quiet Time from John Chapter 1. Finish Lesson 1, if need be, and then start Lesson 2. Again, go through it in the same way with the new believer.

5. **Following Meetings:** After finishing Lesson 2, start asking the new believer to do the next lesson alone, before your next meeting. Assure them that you will help them with whatever isn't clear when you get together. At each meeting, discuss their Quiet Time, lesson answers, questions, other responses, and application of truth to life. Encourage them to invite family and friends to their water baptism, and help them prepare their testimony to give before being baptized. Welcome their guests who come. Sit with them during service, and stay with them until the new believer rejoins them.

6. **TurnAround Lessons:** Prepare new believers to "turn around" and give out by taking them through the lessons on witnessing and discipling. Pray with them to be baptized in the Holy Spirit. Walk them calmly through the process, either in a one-to-one setting or in a small group.

7. **Keep them keeping on!** Enroll new believers in nurturing groups or continue with them one-on-one. Recommended for both settings is *THRIVE – A Handbook for New Christians*, picking up with Lesson 3. (SUS lessons are the same content as THRIVE HNC

Sessions 1-2.) Make sure they get stuck in a web of relationships with brothers and sisters in their new family! That is God's earthly security blanket.

Keep in mind that your goal in discipling is to see the new believer grow in their relationship with Christ, and also to begin to win and disciple others. Remember, Jesus said to teach them to "do all that I have commanded you."

LESSON 1
The Biggest Change in Your Life

How could it happen?

Eternal friendship with you is a gift from **Almighty God**. He has loved you more than you can imagine since long before you were born on earth. So He sent His eternal Son, Jesus Christ, to earth to do the biggest rescue job in history. He is the ONLY person who is able to rescue you from hell (eternal punishment) and make you a child of God. The reason He could do this is because Jesus is also God.

Because He is God, Jesus lived forever in heaven before He was born as a Jewish baby in Israel, 2,000 years ago. Everything Jesus did on earth was good. He lived perfectly to please His Father God and to help others. His life shows you what God is like. He did exactly as God told Him, and always with God's help.

The Roman ruler over Israel executed Jesus at the request of the Jewish leaders, who hated Him because He exposed their sin. They were jealous of Jesus because of the crowds who followed Him. He loved the people, taught them, healed them, and evicted their demons. When Jesus died, God punished Him for all the things every other person did wrong in God's eyes (called "sin," which is living for SELF instead of God and others). (Jesus Himself had nothing to be punished for!)

God brought Jesus back to life from His grave and then brought Him back to heaven in His eternal body to be King of the universe forever. He rules now over every person who *believes* in Him and *willingly obeys* Him. One day

Jesus will return to rule the whole world with love and total authority.

You have heard *about* Jesus, *now you can get to know Him personally!*

If possible, do these lessons with the help of a Christian friend.

INTRODUCTION

You are like a child rescued from drowning and put in a boat that will bring you safely to shore (heaven). Because God loves you, His plan has always been for Jesus to rescue you from going to hell, to bring you to God to be His own child forever.

The New Testament (Bible) tells about Jesus' life. You will need to read in the book called "(The Gospel of) John" to complete these lessons.

1. Jesus rescues you from punishment for disobeying God.

The bad news is: You are guilty of "sin" (disobeying God). The Bible and your conscience make that clear. *Read and fill in.*

- The Good News is: God sent Jesus to remove the _____ that came between you and God. (John, Chapter 1,verse 29.)

- John 3:36 says if you do **not** put your trust in (believe in) Jesus, you will not receive _____ and God's _____ will be forever on you for sinning? Did you know that sin was that bad? _____

- What made God send His Son, Jesus, to earth? (John 3:16-17) _____ How did God "give His Son" for you? _____

- When Jesus was dying on the cross, He *experienced hell* to pay for *your* sins, so you would not have to pay in hell. How does this make you feel toward Jesus? _____

- How do you feel about your selfish actions (sin), knowing that was what Jesus was punished for when he died? _____

- What does John 3:16-18 say you have to do to come to God? _____

- John 6:44 says _____ was pulling _____ to Him, meaning (check one):
  ○ I loved God first. ○ God loved me first.

2. Jesus rescues you to become God's child!

- "To all who received Him (Jesus), He gave the right to become the _____ of _____." (John 1:12)

- To receive Jesus and become God's child, you have to do these 3 things:

  ○ Ask Jesus to forgive your sins and come live in you. (John 1:12)

  ○ Believe in Jesus to be your best Friend (Savior), now and forever. (John 3:16)

  ○ Commit to cooperate with Him daily as your Leader (Lord). (John 15:14)

IF you did all three things, then you are a
child of God and He is your Heavenly Father!

- How does it feel, deep down, to be God's own child?

  _____

- You can now say, "God has put His own Spirit inside of
  _____ to stay (how long?) _____" (John 14:17;
  3:16.) Without your own spirit, your body has no life. With
  God's Spirit living in you, you now have new life!
  (Read again John 3:16-20, and memorize John 3:16.)

3. Think and Thank!— important things to do right now.

- **Think** about what was done for you - and who did it. In
  the space below, write out *John* 3:16, using your name in
  place of the words "world" and "whoever".

  _____

  _____

  _____

  _____

  *(Tell your Christian friend how it feels to see your name
  in this Bible verse.)*

- Now, **thank** Jesus out loud for
  loving you when you were living your own way,
  rescuing you from hell, and for
  coming to **live inside of you** forever.

Talk to Him just like you would talk to a person. Praying is
that simple, and God always hears.

4. Important things to plan ahead and do.

You are now a child of God in God's family with new brothers and sisters. Just like a log burns better when it shares its flame with other logs, you will do better when you share your new life with a spiritual family! God wants you to become an active part of a church that believes the Bible is His message to man. Plan ahead when you will go to church meetings with your Christian friend, and then do as you planned.

CHURCH INFO:

- Plan when and where to meet your Christian friend again for learning and prayer. Try to meet in a day or two. Satan is upset with you, and He will do whatever He can to lead you away from Jesus. When you get tempted to follow Satan again, remember where he will end up! It is important to stay close to Jesus and to keep learning how to get closer. So keep meeting to learn and keep doing what you learn!

In your next lesson, you will begin to learn how to talk to God and know when He is talking to you and what He is saying. The easiest way we can "hear" God talk to us is to read His open letter to everyone, called the Bible. It is an amazing library of 66 books under one cover, arranged in two sections called the "Old Testament" and the "New Testament". Sometimes the New Testament is printed by itself. And remember, whenever your Bible is open, the Author is present!

Each day until your next lesson, read Chapter One in John, after asking God to teach you. Underline the parts that speak to you strongly. Don't worry about the parts you don't understand. You will see and understand new things each time you read. Happy listening! God enjoys talking to you this way. Thank Him, when you read, for the things He shows you - and for just being there for you!

LESSON 2
Talking with God

INTRODUCTION

God's plan is for your new life as a Christian to flow from God—yes, God Himself—living inside of you!
Read John 2:25-3:8

1. God gives you His life after you receive His Son Jesus!

Jesus gives life to your spirit, so He compares Himself to food and drink that gives life to your body. Read John 6:56

- What do you have to do with food and drink before it can give life to your body?

  _____

- What did you do so that Jesus can give life to your spirit?

  _____

- The result, in Jesus' words, is: _____

- You and Jesus can be "in" each other by His _____ being in you. Read John 14:17.

Remember: God is now your loving Heavenly Father and you are His precious child. God may or may not be much like your earthly father. Don't jump to conclusions about God as your Father - let God show you the kind of Father He is. His own Spirit is living in you, so you are always in direct personal contact with God. Being close to God this way calls for continuing conversation with Him as friend with Friend.

2. God wants to talk with you!

Jesus says you have been "born again", because there is new life in you from God's Spirit living in you. That makes you a spiritual newborn baby, who needs to get to know God, your new all-loving Heavenly Father.

Every relationships begins with talking. You were "born again" as a result of talking with God. Here is how it worked. You heard about Jesus from the Bible and began to know that what you heard was true. That was God telling you in your heart. Then you talked to God and asked Him to forgive you and be your Ruler and Friend. The result was your spiritual birth on (date) _____

You get to know someone by being with them and talking with them. God is always with you, and He wants you to hear Him talk to you, and wants you to talk to Him.

- Read in Romans Chapter 8, verses 15-16. This passage says God's _____ is talking to you. What is He saying to you? _____

- Have you felt Him say this to you in your heart?
  ○ Yes ○ No ○ Not sure

- What does He want you to say back to Him? _____

- What do you think God feels toward you as His child, from what you have read in the Bible?
  _____
  _____

- How do you feel toward God, now that you are His child?

_____

3. God created you with the ability to talk with Him

You may be wondering how in this world you can actually talk with God, when God hardly ever talks out loud, and you can't see Him or touch Him.

The first step in learning conversation with God is to set aside for each day a regular time and place to be alone and quiet with God. Start with giving Him your undivided attention for 15-20 minutes. This is a time to talk to God and listen to Him talk to you, as Jesus said in Matthew 6:6. Where and what time each day can you do this?

Time _____ Where _____

In a conversation, the more important person usually talks first. It is important to listen to God before you do a lot of talking. The best way to start listening is by reading and studying God's open letter to us all, the Bible. (Other ways you can increase your understanding of God's written Word is to discuss what you are studying with other Christians, and to hear teaching on the Bible.)

During your daily times to talk with God, do the following:

- Ask God to help you receive His message to you through what you read. What does Jesus promise you in John 14:26? _____

- As you have been reading John, Chapter One, for a few days, did you see new things each time? Did you underline the parts that spoke strongly?

- Now start using the Bible Study Worksheet provided below. Go to the parts you underlined and write the things asked for in the worksheet. Just do your best as you get started on this new project. Your Christian friend will help you.

After listening to God speak to you through His written Word, it is time for you to talk to Him.

■

Date _____

Bible Study Worksheet for John Chapter 1

IMPORTANT THINGS I SEE   HOW THEY APPLY TO MY LIFE

_____   _____

_____   _____

_____   _____

_____   _____

_____   _____

_____   _____

_____   _____

(continue on another sheet)

- In your own words, talk to God (out loud or silently) about the things you wrote about from the chapter you studied.

- Give praise to God for the things about Him you read, and also for what He has done for you and for the ways He is helping you each day.

- Talk to God about whatever else comes to your mind. Be sure to thank Him for coming to live inside of you and for bringing you new (eternal) life! Tell God how wonderful it is for you to be forgiven and to now belong to Him, through having Jesus as your Friend and Leader!

- Also ask Him to help you with the problems you are struggling with. You can also ask Him to help other people with their problems, no matter what those problems are. Remember that God created the whole universe, so He has enough power to do anything. He often heals sickness and injuries, so don't hesitate to ask Him to do things that are impossible for man to do. With God, nothing is impossible!

Remember—Have your time of personal conversation with God each day, and use the Bible Study Worksheet.

4. Time with other people.

It is very important to make time to meet regularly with your Christian friend, who will help explain things and pray for you every day. Also, attend the regular church meetings he/she encourages you to attend. Remember, a log needs other logs to burn well, so get together regularly with other Christians!

Tell the people you usually see from day to day about how Jesus is making a big and wonderful change in your life. Don't argue or try to answer every question. Just tell them what has happened to you. They can't argue with that! These lessons can help you explain.

LESSON 3
Hearing God

INTRODUCTION

God is a totally loving Heavenly Father Who promises to always be with His children.

1. God loves you greatly, and delivers His love directly to you.

- Read Romans 5:5. What are the words in this verse that show that God is generous with His love to you?

  _____

- Where and how does He deliver His love to you?

  _____

2. God always gives you His personal attention.

- God pays such close attention to you that He always knows everything about you in every area of your life. How does Jesus explain it in Luke Chapter 12, verses 6 & 7? _____

- What else does Jesus tell us about God noticing us in Matthew 6:8? _____

- So pray about your problems, knowing that God already knows all about them, He already has a solution, and He has a plan to make it happen. (In Lesson 4, you will see that your actions are part of the solution!)

To do your part in solving your problems, you must know what to do. So "answers" to your prayers very often begin with God talking back to you after you have asked Him to do something, telling you what He wants you to do about the situation. When you do your part by obeying, (showing faith in His guidance) then God will step in and do His part in solving your problem. Reading the Bible is hearing God speak to everyone. The rest of this lesson is to help you learn how to

Hear God Speak to You Individually!

3. Guidelines for HEARING God talk directly to you.

The biggest change that God has planned for your new life with Him is for you to think, feel, speak, and do everything with Him. You will never be alone again, and God doesn't want you to feel or act alone! Doing what He wants depends on first knowing what He wants you to do - and knowing depends on hearing Him tell you. So keep listening, because God keeps talking!

- You have already "heard" God speak to you through the Bible and in your heart, when He made you know that He wanted you to give your life to Him. You obeyed His "voice" then. As you listen now with the desire to obey, God will talk to you about many things.

- Not every spiritual voice is God's. Evil spirits can put thoughts in your mind that make you want to do selfish or destructive things. Any thought or desire that tells you to do something that disagrees with the Bible, or disagrees with what you know about what God is like, is either from your own natural self or from an evil spirit. Tell such thoughts and desires to leave you, because Jesus is your King and you only agree with Him and what He says to do. Read I John 4:1-3 and discuss it with your friend.

• When you read your Bible, sometimes words will seem to "come alive" or "jump off the page" or "burn in your heart". That is God's Spirit taking Bible words written to everyone to tell you something you especially need to know at that time. You should give special attention to obeying what God has said to you with those words. Be sure to also do the other commands you find. Discuss with your Christian friend what God is saying and how to respond.

• Train yourself to speak often with God through each day, until it becomes a habit. He hears your thoughts and feels your feelings. He will remind you of things you read in His written message (the Bible), and He will speak often to you in thoughts and feelings as you "listen" with your heart. You will learn to recognize His "voice" as you continue to listen. His voice will become familiar to you. Isn't that amazing?! Thank God often for being with you and for all He does for you. That will help you stay "tuned in". If God who created everything - including you – is with you all the time giving you his attention, isn't it only right to **give Him your attention**? _____

• Take 15 minutes right now, or at another time you have planned, to have your "Quiet Time" with God as explained in Lesson 2. Listen to Him by studying more of John Chapter 1, and then talk to Him from your heart. Take time to listen for God to talk to you during your praying time, as explained later in this lesson. There is no more wonderful experience in life than having personal talks with eternal God, the Creator of the whole universe - your Heavenly Father!

■

Date _____

Bible Study Worksheet for John Chapter 1

IMPORTANT THINGS I SEE   HOW THEY APPLY TO MY LIFE

_____   _____

_____   _____

_____   _____

_____   _____

_____   _____

_____   _____

_____   _____

(continue on another sheet)

4. "Decisions, Decisions!".

Most of the time it will be easy to know what God wants you to do in each situation by asking yourself: "What does the Bible say about this?", or by thinking: "What could I do to bring honor to Jesus, if people know I am His follower?"

If God wants you to do something that isn't easy to know by asking the above questions, He will tell you what to do, if you listen with your heart and mind. You can ask God right then, "God, what do You want to help me do?" If the thoughts that come into your mind agree with the Bible and bring a peace to your heart, then you can know they are from God. Colossians 3:15 says, "Let the _____ of God rule in your heart". Do what the peaceful thoughts are telling you, and depend on God to help you. Don't act until you have peace in your heart about what you are planning to do.

If you are thinking about doing a specific thing, first ask God, "Can You and I do this together?" If you feel "No Peace" in your heart, then don't do it on your own, apart from God. If you feel peace and a "Yes", then go ahead, depending on God to help you.

An important preparation to being able to hear God's voice clearly is to pray until God places in your heart a desire to just do what HE wants. When that desire is so strong that it blocks out all your natural desires, then you will be able to hear with confidence and go ahead and do what God is saying for you to do.

REMINDER: Continue your DAILY special time of conversation with God. Keep talking with your Christian friend about hearing God speak to you, what you did in response, and what happened as a result (as far as you know). Also, keep attending the regular church meetings and participating in the church activities available to you.

LESSON 4
Obeying God

INTRODUCTION

When God's Spirit joined your spirit, your spirit came alive to live a new way. God intends your new contact with Him to result in new conduct for you. Your old way of living will change to God's way of living as you live your life under His "new management." Read John 15:14.

1. Jesus' contact with His Father produced Jesus' conduct.

- Who decided what Jesus did —
  ○ Jesus or ○ the Father? (John 4:31-34)

- Read John 4:34 and fill in the missing word: Jesus' _____ was to do what His Father wanted Him to do. This means Jesus was "hungry" (wanted) to do what? _____

- How did Jesus know what to do? (John 5:17-20, 30)
  _____

- How was Jesus able to do what He did? (John 5:17; 14:10) _____

2. Your contact with God will produce your conduct.

When human authorities give you commands, they do not personally help you carry out their orders. They want you to do things for them. When God gives commands, He always helps you obey, if you will do what He says with Him! Read John 15:4-5.

- How often does God want you to do something without Him being with you to be your Leader and Partner? (John 15:4-5) _____

- God's works can always be done if you do what he says and trust God to do His part! Write man's part and God's part in these partner miracles:

- John 2:1-11: _____

_____

- John 6:5-13: _____

_____

3. You always have access to God's help.

- Because of your spiritual birth, you were able to enter the _____ of _____. (John 3:3,5)

- God's Spirit in you is ready to help you live your new life God's way. He makes it possible for you to obey your new King, Jesus, Whom you could not obey before. Read John 8:34-36.

    a. Whose slave were you before? _____

    b. Who are you free to obey now? _____

    c. Have you seen any miracles in your life under your new Manager? _____

Thank God for the changes He is already making in your life. Ask Him to help you keep an "attitude of gratitude" toward Him for what He went through so you could change. Be "hungry"(want) to cooperate with the changes He wants to make in your life. How good are the things we naturally prefer to do?

God (like you) enjoys doing things with someone He loves, in this case "_____"! Have you had experiences like Jesus had, as described in John 4:31-34, when you obeyed God and He made you feel good and strong on the inside - like having a spiritual meal? Tell your Christian friend how you feel when you do things with God.

▪

Review: Constant contact/conduct with God is what He wants. Your part is to remember God is with you, giving you His full attention! So pay attention to Him! Talk to Him often, always listen, and do everything with Him and with His help. *Conversation* and *cooperation* are basic to every relationship. Keep both of these activities strong in your relationship with God.

4. Cooperate with God by taking a public stand.

Read Matthew 10:28-39 and see how important it is to go public about getting your life in Jesus. One way of doing this is by being baptized in water. Both Jesus and Peter said _____ should follow faith and repentance. (Mark 16:16; Acts 2:38)

Water baptism is a birthday party, announcing your second birth. By obeying Jesus' command to be baptized, your actions say that life with Jesus means OBEYING Him as King. You are also playing yourself as the main character in a drama, showing on the outside in baptism what has happened to you on the inside. Act I (going under) is the burial of your old self-managed way of life. Act II (coming up) is "startingUP" your new life with Christ. (Romans 6:1-14)

A common and wonderful part of the party is a few words of "testimony" from the persons being baptized about what it means to belong to Jesus. Testimonies bring rejoicing to the spiritual family, who are welcoming new members into God's Kingdom.

God can also use the message of visible action and sincere words to speak into the hearts of unbelievers present, along with the new believers' daily lives continually announcing the change that Jesus can bring to a person's life.(Matthew 5:13-16)

Your big day to be baptized is *(date)*_____.
Don't sell tickets, but do invite family and friends. This is a big deal!

5. Cooperate with God in frequent forgiveness.

You still need forgiveness. Read I John 1:8-9, and thank God for understanding what you need to stay with Him. Whenever you realize that you have acted or spoken apart from God, without giving your attention to God for guidance or without depending on Him, don't allow Satan to discourage you. Read I John 1:5-10. Without delay, do what verse 9 says, which is to _____
What does God always do in response? _____

You need to forgive others to keep being forgiven for your sins.(Matthew 6:12,14-15!) *Don't fail* to practice this VERY important truth!

Remember how much God has forgiven you! Don't stop praying until you can decide to forgive! Keep praying until you can remember the offense without anger and without pain. (For more on forgiveness, see Lesson 9 in *THRIVE – A Handbook for New Christians*)

6. Cooperate with God by loving lost people.

Look at what has happened in your life because people told you about Jesus. Jesus said, "Freely you have received, now freely give." (Matthew 10:8) Here's how to share the Good News.

- Pray and look for opportunities to show kindness. Then look for opportunities to talk about Jesus and what He is doing in you and for you. (Colossians 4:3) The key to doing this is to depend on God's Spirit in you to help you know when to talk about Jesus and what to say. (Matthew 10:19-20) "Try it, you'll like!"(John 4:34-36), and others need it! (Matthew 9:35-36)

- You will notice that thoughts and words often come running into your mind and out of your mouth when you are talking to someone about Jesus. The more you depend on God, the more He helps you listen and say the right things when you talk to people about Him - especially after you have been baptized in the Holy Spirit. (See TurnAround Lesson-Friendship Evangelism.) So step up and speak up! (Acts 1:8)

Congratulations on completing these *StartUp* studies! You have just begun to taste your wonderful new and eternal life with God through Jesus. Be consistent in having your Quiet Time with God. Make your life's ambition to continually grow in knowing Him better and in being and

73

doing what will please Him. Always pursue this goal while staying connected with brothers and sisters in Christ. One day you will stand by yourself before Jesus to give account for your life on earth. Live now to hear Him say then: "Well done, good and faithful servant...Enter into the joy of your Master!"(Matthew 25:21)

A major part of what God wants you to do now is to HELP LOST PEOPLE COME TO HIM, and HELP NEW BELIEVERS STAY WITH HIM, the way others helped you or are helping you. "Freely you have received, freely give!" You can use these same *StartUp Studies* to help others. Read Matthew 28:18-20, and proceed to the TurnAround lessons that follow.

TurnAround Lesson
Friendship Evangelism

Jesus influenced people to believe in Him through loving personal contact. His "witnesses" do the same, with the same preparation as His first disciples - training (to gain understanding and skills), and teamwork with the Holy Spirit (Matthew 28:18-20; Acts 1:8).

TRAINING

Step 1 -**Learn to be a friend to lost persons.** Let God love lost people through you in practical, relational ways! Spend time together. Build a friendship.

Step 2 - Be ready to explain the Gospel in simple words unbelievers can understand.(I Peter 3:15) Keep the following gospel outline and Bible verses in your head as a guide.

Gospel Outline (John 3:16; 1:12; 15:14)

Ask forgiveness from Jesus, your sin-payment (SACRIFICE).

Believe (trust) in Jesus as your helping Friend (SAVIOR).

Cooperate each day with Jesus as your Leader (LORD).

Step 3 - Be ready to obey the Spirit telling you to gently invite your friend to receive Christ. The ABC outline can be used as a guide for them to pray to do that. (Practice explaining to a Christian friend how to pray this kind of prayer, using your own words – as if your friend is a non-believer who wants to begin an eternal relationship with Jesus. Briefly review each kind of faith (ABC) Jesus requires of them - that you discussed before and made sure your friend understands. There should be no last minute surprises introduced before a salvation prayer is prayed.

TEAMWORK

Step 1 - Pray for yourself. Jesus promised, "Follow me and I will make you fishers of men." Jesus baptizes in the Holy Spirit (John 1:33), and the Spirit teams up with you to help you witness about Jesus. (Matthew 10:19-20; Acts 1:6-9; Acts 4:29-31) Does God want you to have this experience? (Acts 2:38-39) Write reasons why?

Acts 2:4 tells how the disciples surrendered to the Spirit so deeply that they praised God in words that the Spirit gave them. When you surrender to the Spirit in the same way, you will also pray with words the Spirit gives you. This will give you faith to team up with the Spirit in witness opportunities, to say and do things beyond your own ability to help other people put their trust in Jesus.

• Read John 7:37-39. Jesus invites you to come to Him and "drink", IF you are "_____". How "thirsty" are you? Do you want to be filled (baptized) in the Holy Spirit? Why?

• To be baptized in the Spirit, you have to surrender to the Spirit. Ask Jesus to show you if you are holding back from the Spirit's control in any way that will hinder your being baptized in the Holy Spirit, and what you should do about it. Promise God to do it, and tell someone who will hold you accountable.

- Now ask Jesus to baptize you in His Holy Spirit (John 1:33). Your part is to surrender completely so the Spirit can take control. Begin to surrender your voice in praising Jesus out loud with joy (Luke 24:52-53) because He has saved you and IS going to baptize you in His Holy Spirit. He promised (Luke 11:9-13; Acts 2:38-39) - so thank Him, because you trust Him to do what He says!

- As you praise Him, concentrate completely on Jesus the Baptizer. He will make you know in your heart (give you FAITH) that if you will begin to speak, the Spirit will give you the words. (Acts 2:4:"They began to speak...as the Spirit was giving them (words).") When the faith comes, you begin to speak - but don't use your own words. Just relax in faith and say what the Spirit gives you. Praying this way will soon feel very natural. This experience is a BEGINNING...so continue it daily! The more you and the Holy Spirit team up, the better you will work together.

Step 2 - Praying for lost people.

- The Spirit will guide you to lost persons He wants you to influence (Acts 8:29). Two are named:_____

_____

- Pray for the Spirit to give you His love for non-followers and seek friendship with them. (Galatians 5:22-23)

- Pray for ability from the Spirit to do and say what will help them come to Him. (Acts1:8)

- Pray for the Spirit to open their heart to receive Him. (Acts16:14)

Step 3 - Team up for prayer. (Matthew 18:19-20)

Choose one or two Christian friends to be partners with you in praying for each other to lead lost friends to Jesus.

• Exchange the names of those you are praying for.

Partner _____ Their lost friend _____

Partner _____ Their lost friend _____

• Pray for each other for the Holy Spirit's help with love, deeds, and words, and for Him to open the hearts of lost friends.

• Contact each other weekly for progress reports, mutual encouragement, prayer together, and to celebrate when someone comes to faith in Christ.

For the TurnAround Lesson on being a Discipling Friend, go back to page 47.

One last question: If you win and disciple one person this year, and then next year your disciplee wins and disciples one person and you win and disciple another, and the next year the four of you win and disciple one person each...and this process continues for ten years – how many would be added to God's eternal family? Do the math:

_1_ + _1_ = __; __ + __ = __; __ + __ = __; __ + __ = __; __ + __ = __;

__ + __ = __; __ + __ = __; __ + __ = __; __ + __ = __;

___ + ___ = _____!   "If we slow down, we can go faster!"

For compelling insight into every believer's call to ministry, I highly recommend:

Idle in the Marketplace at the Eleventh Hour, by David Robinson (City Limits International Publishing; 2012)

(excerpts)

The mission of the Church goes far beyond having better members and services to provide community acts of benevolence. Those are worthy endeavors, but should not be the extent of her mandate and influence. Those are byproducts of the Church's real mission. Her biblical mandate in Matthew 28 is to go into the entire world (to make disciples), including the marketplace, government and education... What is the Father's business in these three entities? To lead and influence the leadership in all three - if not, evil will take its place. The Church cannot afford to be idle at the eleventh hour.

Business in the marketplace creates the economy. It pays for everything in all three entities. Extending the Kingdom, discipling nations, and spreading the Gospel takes massive amounts of resources today, as does any large endeavor. Every dollar the Church invests in this effort comes from the marketplace...

Government is the second entity the Church needs to influence. (Government) passes laws and regulations that control the society of every nation...America is suffering from moral aids and ethical decay at every level...

The educational arena determines the values and philosophies of every generation...We are in dire need of Spirit-filled leaders having the intellectual credentials, passion to contend for the faith, and willingness to do battle for the educational institutions in America.

(available on Amazon.com)

New Christian Life Materials
by James H. Hall

THRIVE

Discipler's Guide..$20
- ☐ Gives complete instructions for one-to-one or small-group discipling of new Christians
- ☐ Can be used individually for self-help instruction or for training disciplers
- ☐ New-Christian discipling sessions included with answers and Discipler Helps

Handbook for New Christians...$14
- ☐ Fifteen reproducible sessions for mentoring new Christians until they can win and mentor others
- ☐ Session worksheets guide new Christians to the milk of the Word, to learn how to live in daily conversation and cooperation with Jesus

StartUp Studies...$4
- ☐ Four lessons adapted from Sessions 1 and 2 in the THRIVE - Handbook for New Christians, plus guidelines for evangelism/discipling (35 pages, 8.5 in. x 5.5 in.)

SENT to your neighbors!.......................... Paperback $5/eBook $4
- ☐ Explains a "soft-sell" witness style to empower rank and file believers to influence toward Christ lost persons in their personal harvest fields to whom they are sent by the Sent One, Jesus. (86 pages, 8.5 in. x 5.5 in.)

To order materials and/or schedule ministry
www.newchristian.com   E-mail: JHHalls@aol.com

Rev. James H. Hall, New Christian Life Ministries
1411 E. Stoneridge St. • Springfield, MO 65803
Phone: 417-833-9052 • Fax: 417-833-1142

Shipping and handling:
$1.00 to $49.99—15 percent; over $50—10 percent

Make checks payable to **NCLM**.
Credit card orders: www.newchristian.com